LESLIE STEPHEN

LESLIE STEPHEN

by

DESMOND MacCARTHY

THE LESLIE STEPHEN LECTURE DELIVERED
BEFORE THE UNIVERSITY OF CAMBRIDGE
ON 27 MAY 1937

CAMBRIDGE
AT THE UNIVERSITY PRESS
1937

CAMBRIDGE
UNIVERSITY PRESS

University Printing House, Cambridge CB2 8BS, United Kingdom

Published in the United States of America by Cambridge University Press, New York

Cambridge University Press is part of the University of Cambridge.

It furthers the University's mission by disseminating knowledge in the pursuit of education, learning and research at the highest international levels of excellence.

www.cambridge.org
Information on this title: www.cambridge.org/9781107635142

© Cambridge University Press 1937

First published 1937
First paperback edition 2014

A catalogue record for this publication is available from the British Library

ISBN 978-1-107-63514-2 Paperback

LESLIE STEPHEN

In that joyously affectionate and informal book, *The Life and Letters of Leslie Stephen*, Maitland, after disclaiming any intention of criticising his work, says: "If, as I doubt not, he has left worthy successors, someone will some day do for him what he to our admiration did for many others; illustrate in a small compass his life by his books, his books by his life and both by their environment. Meanwhile," he says, "here are some materials."

And this, as perhaps you guess, is what I would like to do. But even were I a "worthy successor" in other ways, I should be hard put to it to succeed without Leslie Stephen's gift of concision. To place his books in their environment would mean giving an account of the struggle in the 'seventies and 'eighties between Orthodoxy and Free-thought, in which Leslie Stephen played so effective a part, and it would mean giving some historical account of that close alliance between Agnosticism and Puritanism, as noticeable in him as it was in Huxley, which has struck a later generation as curious. That alliance was certainly not adopted by them as a defence against those who argued that attacks upon the Scriptures undermined morality; though Huxley's and Leslie Stephen's strenuous moral orthodoxy did have a protective value. The connection between their Agnosticism and Puritanism had deeper root. After all, the desire to eradicate beliefs which seem false or groundless is a moral passion; and when that has shown itself strong enough to make a man face odium, we need not be surprised to find he is a staunch moralist all round. Neither Huxley nor Leslie Stephen were sceptics; they were certain of too many things, and their adversaries were fair, I think, when they said that their "agnosticism" was accompanied by little doubt about the non-existence of God. The term "agnostic" was coined by Huxley; but Maitland is of the

(6)

opinion that it was the controversial writings of Leslie Stephen which gave it vogue.

Judged by the influence upon men's minds alone, the writings which Leslie Stephen collected in *Essays on Free-thinking and Plain-speaking* (1873), and in *An Agnostic's Apology* (1893) (most of the latter written much earlier), must be considered the most important part of his life's work. One reason why, as we shall be presently reminded, he wrote disparagingly of literary criticism, was that it seemed so trivial compared with criticism of thought and religion. What if he had induced some readers to take a clearer view of the merits and limitations of Fielding or De Quincey, or if he had succeeded in giving a tolerably true account of some man's life? Of what importance was that compared with helping men to a truer conception of the nature of things, or with the work of a man of science? This reflection, which often visited him, robbed him of retrospective satisfaction in his books, though while writing them he derived keen pleasure from knocking nails on the head. He knew that his controversial writings had made an impression on the public, who think by fits and starts, but before the end of the nineteenth century his controversial work was over. He could have only repeated himself.

Among go-between thinkers of that century who disseminated ideas without originating them, he must be reckoned among the three first—I cannot think of a fourth comparable in influence to set beside Huxley, Matthew Arnold and Leslie Stephen. I except Herbert Spencer, because he was a system-maker. W. K. Clifford died too young and wrote too little: the wide influence of Samuel Butler came later and was chiefly posthumous. But Arnold had his poetry to show, Huxley his scientific work as a Zoologist. What else of value outside controversy had Leslie Stephen achieved?

I will try to answer that question which he often put despondently to himself; to describe the kind of criticism he wrote, and, using also external evidence, the man who was behind it. This was his own way of setting about criticism; indeed, the most comprehensive description of Leslie Stephen as a critic would be to call him an expert in character, if that is also taken as implying connoisseurship in defining points of view. It is his conception of the writer that gives unity to most of his literary essays; not the relation of a book to the history of literature or to some standard of perfection. What he investigated with greater interest was the relation of a book to its author. Of course, this did not preclude his pointing out with great acuteness, as he went along, an author's successes or failures as a craftsman, or reminding us of the pertinence or the folly of a work as a commentary on life; but as a critic he directed our attention chiefly to the sort of man the author had apparently been; to the man who saw and felt things thus and thus, and expressed himself in this way and no other.

The title of his last four volumes of criticism, *Studies of a Biographer*, is in no small degree applicable to his first collection of critical essays, *Hours in a Library*. In his essay on "Shakespeare the Man", we find him writing:

"Now I confess that to me one main interest in reading is always the communion with the author. *Paradise Lost* gives me the sense of intercourse with Milton, and the *Waverley Novels* bring me a greeting from Scott. Every author, I fancy, is unconsciously his own Boswell, and, however 'objective' or dramatic he professes to be, really betrays his own secrets. Browning is one of the authorities against me. If Shakespeare, he says, really unlocked his heart in the sonnets, why 'the less Shakespeare he'. Browning declines for his part to follow the example, and fancies that he has preserved his privacy. Yet we must, I think, agree with a critic who emphatically declares that a main characteristic of Browning's own poetry is that it brings us into contact with the real 'self of the author'. Self-revelation is not the less clear because involuntary or quite incidental to the main purpose of a book. I may read Gibbon simply to learn facts; but I enjoy his literary merits because I recognise my friend of the autobiography who 'sighed as a lover and obeyed as a son'. I may study Darwin's *Origin of Species* to clear my views upon natural selection; but as a book it interests me even through the defects of style by the occult personal charm of the candid, sagacious, patient seeker for truth. In pure literature the case is, of course, plainer, and I will not count up instances because, in truth, I can hardly think of a clear exception. Whenever we know a man adequately we perceive that, though different aspects of his character may be made prominent in his life and his works, the same qualities are revealed in both, and we cannot describe the literary without indicating the personal charm."

Now a critic who approaches his subjects in this spirit will inevitably discourse more about human nature and morals than about art, and Leslie Stephen is the least aesthetic of noteworthy critics. In this connection his strenuous evangelical upbringing must not be overlooked; through both his father and his mother his home was affiliated to the Clapham Sect. He is constantly harping on "sincerity". Sincerity is a condition of all satisfactory personal relations, and therefore a condition of the communion between writer and reader which he valued most. In his essay on Sterne, whom he finds deficient in that respect, he says:

"The qualification must, of course, be understood that a great book really expresses the most refined essence of the writer's character. It gives the author transfigured and does not represent all the stains and distortions which he may have received in his progress through the world. In real life we might have been repelled by Milton's stern Puritanism, or by some outbreak of rather testy self-assertion. In reading *Paradise Lost*, we feel only the loftiness of character, and are raised and inspirited by the sentiments without pausing to consider the particular application.

"If this be true in some degree of all imaginative writers, it is especially true of humorists. For humour is essentially the expression of a personal idiosyncrasy.... We love the humour in short so far as we love the character from which it flows."

He could not bring himself to love Sterne, which I (though love may be too strong a word) find no difficulty in doing. He examined his life, especially his married life and his flirtations, with severity, and he concluded that "Sterne was a man who understood to perfection the art of enjoying his own good feelings as a luxury without humbling himself to translate them into practice" (Stephen's definition of a sentimentalist). The judgment pronounced by Thackeray on Sterne seemed to him substantially unimpeachable. He strongly reprobated Sterne's trick of inclining our thoughts (before we realise it) gently towards indecency. With that sense of fun which delights to trip up the dignity of the reader, trusting to his smiling afterwards, he had no sympathy. Leslie Stephen did not smile at that sort of mischief; nor did he make any comment on the really penetrating humour of the opening of *Tristram Shandy*.

Nevertheless, it must not be supposed that this essay, perhaps more likely than any other in *Hours in a Library* to strike our contemporaries as missing the point, is without warmly appreciative passages. Referring to Sterne's touches of exquisite precision, he says that "they give the impression that the thing has been done once for all". Two or three of the scenes in which Uncle Toby expresses his sentiments struck him as being "as perfect in their way as the half-dozen lines in which Mrs Quickly describes the end of Falstaff; and Uncle Toby's oath", he declares to be "a triumph fully worthy of Shakespeare"; but he adds, "the recording angel, though he comes in effectively, is a little suspicious to me". While admitting the felicity with which the scene is presented, he suggests that it would have been really stronger had the angel been omitted (by stronger, he means more moving), "for the angel seems to introduce an unpleasant air as of eighteenth-century politeness; we fancy that he would have welcomed a Lord Chesterfield to the celestial mansions with a faultless bow and a dexterous compliment".

Perfectly true. But to wish on that account the angel away is surely to miss the point of

Sterne, whose attitude towards all emotions was playful. No doubt Sterne thought that here, or in the bravura passage on the dead donkey, he was achieving the acme of pathos. But his temperament was stronger than any conscious intention; consequently what in effect we enjoy, as everywhere in Sterne, is an elegant ambiguity. As with some other Irishmen known to fame, Sterne's heart was in his imagination. The infection we catch from him is, as Goethe noticed, a light fantastic sense of freedom; a state of mind (Shandyism) in which we enjoy together the pleasures of extravagant sensibility, and a feeling that nothing much matters.

Leslie Stephen's attitude towards Sterne's pathetic passages was the same as Dr Johnson's who, when Miss Monckton said: "I am sure they have affected me", replied smiling and rolling himself about, "That is because, dearest, you are a dunce." Johnson set no store by airy detachment, nor could he believe that posterity would cherish its products. Did he not point to Sterne as an instance of the ephemeral nature of all reputations founded on the fantastic? Leslie Stephen had no sense of the fantastic, or of the charm of the artificial; it is one of the dumb notes on his piano. He wanted to be moved; and more—he wanted to be certain that the author had been moved himself.

"We are always pursued in reading Pope", he says, "by disagreeable misgivings. We don't know what comes from the heart, and what from the lips: when the real man is speaking, and when we are only listening to old commonplaces skilfully vamped.... A critic of the highest order is provided with an Ithuriel spear, which discriminates the sham sentiments from the true. As a banker's clerk can tell a bad coin by its ring on the counter, without need of a testing apparatus, the true critic can instinctively estimate the amount of bullion in Pope's epigrammatic tinsel. But criticism of this kind, as Pope truly says, is as rare as poetical genius. Humbler writers must be content to take their weights and measures, or, in other words, to test their first impression, by such external evidence as is available. They must proceed cautiously in these delicate matters, and instead of leaping to the truth by a rapid intuition, patiently enquire what light is thrown upon Pope's sincerity by the recorded events of his life, and a careful cross-examination of the various witnesses to his character."

Leslie Stephen did not trust himself to tell good coin by its ring, or perhaps it would be truer to say he thought he ought not to. Certainly, investigations into the genuineness of an author require a testing apparatus, even when conducted by a critic of rapid intuitions. In the case of Pope that investigation ended unfavourably. I will not consider at this point how far that verdict ought to modify our estimate of Pope's poetry, but will turn to an instance where the results of a similar enquiry were so overwhelmingly favourable that they reversed a judgment based on the written word. In his first essay on Johnson, Leslie Stephen wrote:

"The whole art of criticism consists in learning to know the human being who is partially revealed to us in his spoken or his written words. Whatever the means of communication, the problem is the same. The two methods of enquiry may supplement each other; but their substantial agreement is the test of their accuracy. If Johnson, as a writer, appears to us to be a mere windbag and manufacturer of sesquipedalian verbiage, whilst as a talker, he appears to be one of the most genuine and deeply feeling of men, we may be sure that our analysis has been somewhere defective."

Johnson was the man after Leslie Stephen's heart. Of his five biographical monographs in the *English Men of Letters*, his Johnson is the best, and it is equal to the very best in that excellent series. Johnson was the man he loved most in literature, though not (need it be said?) the writer he admired most, which incidentally throws some doubt on his critical method. Johnson as a writer seemed to him "a great force half wasted because the fashionable costume of the day hampered the free exercise of his powers"; but Johnson as he is known through the records of his life and his talk, embodied nearly all the qualities which Leslie Stephen admired most in other writers.

We cannot be in Johnson's company long without becoming aware that what attracts us to him so strongly is that he combined a disillusioned estimate of human nature, sufficient to launch twenty little cynics, with a craving for love and sympathy so urgent that it would have turned a weaker nature into a benign sentimentalist, and in a lesser degree this is what attracts us in Leslie Stephen. His raciest passages might often be described as cynical. There are also evidences of deep feeling. There is a Johnsonian contempt for those who look only upon the bright side of life or human nature, equalled only by a contempt for those who adopt a querulous or dainty tone.

"Good sense," he says, "is one of the excellent qualities to which we are scarcely inclined to do justice at the present day; it is the guide of a time of equilibrium, stirred by no vehement gales of passion, and we lose sight of it just when it might give us some useful advice."

But he is aware of its limitations. "Like all the shrewd and sensible part of mankind", he says of Johnson, "he condemns as mere moonshine what may be easily the first faint dawn of new daylight." That is an important admission.

But Leslie Stephen was born in 1832, not 1709, which implies considerable differences, and allowing for those, it is tempting to describe his critical work as an attempt to go on writing, in the nineteenth century, Johnson's *Lives of the Poets*. He was more at home with prose writers; but the poets he did study were Pope, Crabbe, Coleridge, Wordsworth, Tennyson and Matthew Arnold; Shelley in so far as his poetry is related to the ideas of Godwin; Cowper in so far as he could be compared with Rousseau, and Donne—but only in relation to his times. He sees Pope as "the incarnation of the literary spirit", and as the complete antithesis to the evil principle of dullness which generates an atmosphere in which literature cannot thrive; but he would be the last man to see in such a phrase as "die of a rose in aromatic pain" the best evidence of Pope's genius.

The essays on Tennyson and Matthew Arnold contain little literary criticism. The former gives an account of what Tennyson's poetry meant to Stephen's generation, and shows a strong preference for the earlier poetry.

"I cannot", he wrote, "though my inability may be owing to my spiritual blindness, place him among 'the great sage poets', but I have wished to intimate that such as I am are not therefore disqualified from appreciating his poetry in another capacity: as a document indicating the effect of modern movements of thought upon a mind of extraordinary delicacy and a nature of admirable sweetness; but, far more, as a perfect utterance of emotions which are all equally beautiful in themselves whatever the 'philosophy' with which they are associated."

He utterly repudiated (and how rightly!) Taine's verdict on *In Memoriam* as the mourning of a correct gentleman wiping away his tears with a cambric handkerchief; but he regretted that the poet should be always haunted by the fear of depriving his "sister of her happy views" ("a woefully feeble phrase, by the way, for Tennyson"), and perpetually be praising the philosopher for keeping his doubts to himself.

"Noble poetry, let us admit, may express either faith or scepticism:...but Tennyson, even in the *In Memoriam*, always seems to me to be like a man clinging to a spar left floating after a shipwreck, knowing that it will not support him, and yet never able to make up his mind to strike out and take his chance of sinking or swimming."

In the essay on Arnold he expresses the same impatience at being told again and again, however melodiously, that the wisest of us must take dejectedly "his seat upon the intellectual throne", keeping as our only friend "sad patience, too near neighbour to despair".

"This note jars upon some people who prefer, perhaps, the mild resignation of the *Christian Year*. I fail of sympathy for the opposite reason. I cannot affect to share Arnold's discomfort.

I have never been able—doubtless it is a defect —to sympathise with the Obermanns and Amiels whom Arnold admired; excellent but surely effeminate persons, who taste of the fruit of the Tree of Knowledge, and finding the taste bitter, go on making wry faces over it all their lives; and admitting with one party that old creeds are doomed, assert with the other that all beauty must die with them....I say all this simply as explaining why the vulgar— including myself—fail to appreciate these musical moans over spilt milk, which represent rather a particular eddy in an intellectual revolution than the deeper and more permanent emotions of human nature."

It is impossible to imagine a Matthew Arnold who had never been at Oxford and a Leslie Stephen who had never been at Cambridge. The stamp which this University left on him was lasting. The fourteen years he spent here as an undergraduate and a fellow of Trinity Hall, from 1850 to 1864, decided what he was to admire and trust in men and books throughout his life. A famous definition might be modified to fit him: Criticism is the adventures of the soul of Cambridge among masterpieces. Souls like bodies change. Perhaps that of Cambridge has changed or is changing; from time to time indications of that possibility have lately reached me. All I can say is that the spirit of Cambridge in the late 'nineties was very like indeed to that which Leslie Stephen knew and carried away with him. He was well aware that some of these adventures might cause outsiders to blaspheme, and there is a recurring note in his criticism—I will not call it apologetic, it was often humorously defiant—which amounts now and then to an admission that possibly the soul of Cambridge had no business at all to embark on such adventures; to risk perdition in regions where reason is at a disadvantage compared with intuition, and the habits are encouraged of skimming over intellectual difficulties, and deviating into the delicate impertinences of egotism. As a practising critic he limited himself as far as he could to that aspect of his subject about which it was possible to argue. He was a man of letters who would have preferred to be a philosopher or a man of science. His moving essay on Wordsworth was, as its title "Wordsworth's Ethics" suggests, chiefly a commentary on the poet's thought and the value of his poetry to those in sorrow.

"Other poetry becomes trifling when we are making our inevitable passage through the Valley of the Shadow of Death. Wordsworth's alone retains its power." The essay was written shortly after the death of his first wife, Thackeray's daughter, in 'seventy-five; and together with the beautiful description of "The Alps in Winter" and "The Agnostic's Apology" (not the book of that name, but the essay in it), it might be considered Leslie Stephen's *De Profundis*, or rather, as Maitland says, his "*in excelsis*". Those three essays contain the passages which let us most unreservedly into his innermost feelings. In "An Agnostic's Apology" he speaks as one acquainted with grief:

"Standing by an open grave, and moved by all the most solemn sentiments of our nature, we all, I think—I can only speak for myself with certainty—must feel that the Psalmist takes his sorrow like a man, and as we, with whatever difference of dialect, should wish to take our own sorrows; while the Apostle is desperately trying to shirk the inevitable and at best resembles the weak comforters who try to cover up the terrible reality under a veil of well-meant fiction. I would rather face the inevitable with open eyes."

In the closing passage of "The Alps in Winter" he comes down to the matter of fact, to the *buffet* and the railway station. "The winter Alps no longer exist. They are but a vision—a faint memory intruding itself at intervals, when the roar of the commonplace has an interval of stillness. Only, if dreams were not at times the best and most solid of realities, the world would be intolerable." That abrupt turn at the end, after he has been modulating into the matter of fact out of the nearest approach he ever allowed himself to impassioned description, is characteristic.

The provinces of the poet and philosopher

were in his view concentric but not coincident, and the poetry he felt best able to criticise was that kind which could be most directly reconverted from an expression of emotion into thought. But he was well aware that this was not all that was required of a critic of poetry.

"Our best critics of poetry", he wrote, "at least, from Dryden to Matthew Arnold, have been (to invert a famous maxim) poets who have succeeded. Coleridge's specific merit was not, as I think, that he laid down any scientific theory. I don't believe that any such theory has as yet any existence except in embryo. He was something almost unique in this as in his poetry, first because his criticism (so far as it was really excellent) was the criticism of love, the criticism of a man who combined the first single impulse of admiration with the power of explaining why he admired; and secondly, and as a result, because he placed himself at the right point of view."

Leslie Stephen, for his part, was well aware of the danger, though he did not always avoid it, of applying strong sense to inappropriate topics, and falling into the error of Johnson in his criticism of *Lycidas* and Gray.

His first impulses of admiration he seldom felt able to analyse, and nothing would induce him merely to "shriek and clasp his hands in ecstacy". And yet from childhood he had been particularly susceptible to poetry, and few men have been able to repeat more of it by heart. He was one of the fortunates who do not need to learn verse that has delighted them; and it was a persistent habit of his to rumble it out on his solitary walks, which in one of his gaunt abstruse appearance was apt to startle passers-by. As a child, poetry and such books as the *Arabian Nights* had often excited him to a degree, alarming his parents; and since he was both nervously shy and deplorably feeble in physique, his early education was deliberately planned to correct an extreme sensibility. It was while at Cambridge that he changed physically and temperamentally, first into an enthusiastic oar, then into a rowing-coach famous for his wind on the towing path, and incidentally into one of the first Alpine climbers and long-distance walkers of his day. In mind he became an almost fanatical admirer of intellect, and a mathematician. He also became a clergyman, but for several years he was so entirely absorbed in his life as a fellow and tutor of Trinity Hall that he did not realise the falseness of his position.

"I had taken orders", he wrote in *Some Early Impressions*, "rashly, though not, I trust, with conscious insincerity, on a sort of tacit understanding that Maurice or his like would act as an interpreter of the true facts.... It may be easy to read any meaning into a dogma, but since allegorising has gone out of fashion, historical narratives are not so malleable. They were, it seemed to me, true or false, and could not be both at once. Divines, since that day, have discovered that it is possible to give up the history without dropping a belief in revelation. I could not then, as I cannot now, take that view. I had to give up my profession. I once heard an anecdote of Maurice which proves, I think, that he was not without humour. He was lecturing a class of young men

(29)

upon the Old Testament, and came to the story of Jacob's questionable behaviour to Esau. After noticing the usual apologies, he added: 'After all, my brethren, this story illustrates the tendency of the spiritual man in all ages to be a liar and a sneak.' Nobody, it is superfluous to add, was less of a liar or a sneak than Maurice. But the 'tendency' may lead the spiritual man to do quite innocently what in other men can only be done by deliberate self-mystification. I, not being a spiritual man, must have deserved one or both of these epithets had I continued to set forth as solemn truths narratives which I could not spiritualise and which seemed to me to be exploded legends implying a crude and revolting morality—I gave up the attempt to reconcile the task to my conscience....By degrees I gave up a good deal more; and here I must make a further confession. Many admirable people have spoken of the agony caused by the abandonment of their old creed. Truth has forced them to admit that the very pillars upon which their whole superstructure of faith rested are unsound. The shock has caused them exquisite pain, and even if they have gained a fresh basis for a theory of life, they still look back fondly at their previous state of untroubled belief. I have no such story to tell. In truth, I did not feel that the solid ground was giving way beneath my feet, but rather that I was being relieved of a cumbrous burden. I was not discovering that my creed was false, but that I had never really believed it."

That confession is significant. His faith, while he possessed it, had not been accompanied by what is called spiritual life. He had never associated religion with his most valued emotions towards nature or man. The points at which he had touched Christianity had been purely moral; and these he took over intact into his new life: they were a contempt, not to say dread, of self-indulgence, a belief in the importance of chastity, and something approaching adoration for tenderness of heart, while his reprobation of the softer vices remained adamant.

In 1862 he resigned his tutorship by refusing to take services in Chapel, and in 1867 his fellowship. Then he began to earn a living in London as a journalist. He had lingered on at

Cambridge those last two years because the atmosphere of the place was singularly sympathetic to him. "The one thing", he says, "that can spoil the social intercourse of well-educated men living in great freedom from unnecessary etiquette is a spirit of misplaced zeal"; and from that Cambridge was blessedly free. There were also no prophets; prophets, though not necessarily humbugs in themselves, were apt, he thought, to be the cause of humbug in others. In his essay on Jowett, and elsewhere, he has contrasted the spirit of Cambridge with that of Oxford:

"We had some very vigorous and excellent tutors, but they were rather anxious to disavow than to assert any such personal influence as is independent of downright logical argument. Perhaps this was partly due to the mathematical turn of Cambridge studies. At the time when Oxford was dimly troubled by the first rumours about German theology, Cambridge reformers were chiefly concerned to introduce a knowledge of the new methods of mathematical analysis, to which Englishmen had been blinded by a superstitious reverence for Newton. That was an excellent aim; but of course you cannot appeal to men's 'souls' in the name of the differential calculus. Even when Cambridge men took to the study of classical literature, they stuck to good, tangible matters of grammatical construction without bothering themselves about purely literary or philosophical interests. They did not deny the existence of the soul; but knew that it should be kept in its proper place. It may be an estimable entity; but it also generates 'fads' and futile enthusiasms and gushing sentimentalisms. It should not be unduly stimulated in early years, but kept in due subordination to the calm understanding occupied with positive matters of fact."

What he valued most at Cambridge were the friendships which spring from discussion; in the pursuit of truth he allowed the soul full play. He would also have agreed with Mr Belloc that in youth, the essence of University life is "laughter and the love of friends". In a volume of essays on Sports edited by Anthony Trollope (1868), the

(33)

article on "Rowing" is almost certainly by Leslie Stephen; and there the writer speaking of fellowship among oarsmen says: "To my mind, the pleasantest of all such bonds are those which we form with fellow students by talking nonsense with them and mistaking it for philosophy." Possibly, as an undergraduate, he was regarded by his most intellectual contemporaries as a "rowing rough".

It was a great regret to him that, unlike his brother FitzJames, he was, unfortunately, not chosen by the Cambridge Apostles to be one of them.

Perhaps this is the place to say something about his intellectual ambitions. Their nature as well as the direction of them had an effect on his criticism. Apparently he was not ambitious, but he was only not ambitious because, in literature at any rate, he thought only the highest achievement worth while; and that was out of his reach. One friend attributed to him the opinion that on the whole books ought *not* to be written; and there is occasionally something in the tone of his comments on authors which lends plausibility to that exaggeration. He would have gladly extended the condemnation of mediocre poetry ("In poetry there is no golden mean; mediocrity there is of a different metal") to every branch of literature. Yet he lived in a period of hero-worship, and was himself extremely susceptible to emotions of enthusiasm and reverence. His horror of gush was partly due to fear of failing to do justice to those almost sacred feelings. He held (and this was one of his first principles as a critic) that "a man's weakness can rarely be overlooked without underestimating his strength". Some of his studies in human nature might seem grudging, owing to the number of reservations they contain, until the reader has grasped that praise from Leslie Stephen, which he always strove to make precise, meant a very great deal.

His essays are an effective protest against the contemporary habit of debasing the currency of praise. He was absurdly humble about his own writings, partly, as I have said, because he would have far rather been a philosopher or a man of science, partly on account of this sense of the width of the gap between work of the first order and the next. It is possible that a tendency to dwell on that gap was self-consolatory; if he could be by no means reckoned among writers of the first order, others of no mean merit were likewise excluded. But only a constitutional diffidence, or, as he sometimes was inclined to suspect, an inverted conceit, can account for his humility in some directions. He even compared his own writing, with a sigh of inferiority, to that of John Morley, whose style, though it may have the appearance at a distance of marble, in texture resembles blancmange. At any rate you cannot poke holes in Leslie Stephen's page with an umbrella. There is no doubt he was a self-disappointed man. His editorship of the *Cornhill Magazine* gave him leisure to try his hand intermittently at solving the old Utilitarian problem of reconciling "the general Happiness" with the principle of a rational egotism, and at proving that the "good" had a survival value for society, though not necessarily for the individual. Many years afterwards, his daughter, Virginia Woolf, asked him which was his favourite among his books; all he would reply was that he knew which one he would like the world to think his best—*The Science of Ethics*. The reception of it disappointed him. Sidgwick, reviewing it in *Mind*, showed that he did not think the book had solved any of the difficulties he had raised himself in *The Methods of Ethics*. No second edition was ever called for. It was a work which had occupied Stephen off and on for six years. It was published in 1882, and, as the *Cornhill* was flagging at that time, his disappointment made him accept the editorship of *The Dictionary of National Biography*. He did not embark on this incalculably beneficent task with much enthusiasm. He describes it as "a very laborious and what was worse, a very worrying piece of work", and at the start the work was unfamiliar to him. He was not a researcher by inclination and he had not estimated the burden involved. "I thought I should have time for other things and hoped the *Dictionary* would either die at once or make such a success that I might be able to content myself with superintending it and have a second-in-command." He had a dangerous collapse in 1888. Volume xxɪɪ of the *Dictionary* was published in 1890 with Sidney Lee's name also on the title page, who had been his sub-editor from the start. This joint editorship continued till the twenty-seventh volume when, after an attack of influenza, Leslie Stephen resigned. How did he regard an achievement which has proved as important to our culture, as any recent scientific discovery to our comfort? He admits he "came to take a certain pride in it"; but it evidently did not relieve that sense of failure which haunted him. After the death of his second wife, Mrs Duckworth, while he could think of nothing but the past, he wrote a long confidential letter to his children. In substance this document is an account of the two women he had loved, but it contains passages about himself. Writing of his children's mother he says:

"When I walked into a room with her, I used to say to myself, everybody must see that she is the noblest woman present. And she took pride in me! Alas and alas again! Did I deserve it? Does it matter? But of that pride I must say something. I used often to complain of my work. I see that I told her in my early letters that I felt myself to be painfully inferior to Morley for example, and in later years, I constantly told her that I was 'a failure'. That became a kind of proverb between us. Now, partly for my own sake, I think it right to tell you what my feeling about myself really is. I know, of course, that I am a man of ability— literary at any rate. I feel myself to be really in this superior to many more popular writers. I have received many high compliments from good judges. When I think (as my Julia used to tell me I might think) of the way in which my friends spoke of me, of Lowell and Norton and Croom Robertson and Sidgwick and Morley and G. Meredith and Morison and many others, I feel ungrateful in making my complaints: I am not a failure pure and simple: I am, I hold, a failure in this way: I have scattered myself over too many subjects. I think that I had it in me to write something which should make a real mark in ethical and philosophical speculation. Unluckily, what with journalism and the *Dictionary*, I have been too much of a Jack-of-all-trades, and instead of striking home in any one direction, have shown (as my friends admitted) capacity for striking. I don't think that this matters very much, as you shall see, but I do feel that if the history of English thought in this century should ever be written, my name will come in a footnote and small type, whereas, if my energies had been better directed, it might have occupied a paragraph, even a section of a chapter, in full-sized type. The cause is that want of self-confidence which I indicated as an early failing.

"Well, I say this once for all, in order to explain her feeling about it. She used to ridicule me for my excessive modesty; though I hope that she did not dislike it. I used, I must confess, and sometimes I confessed to her the truth, to exaggerate my self-humiliation in order to extort from her some of her delicious compliments. They were delicious, for even if they implied error of judgment, they implied the warmest love. Though she knew that I was 'fishing for compliments', she would not find it in her heart to refuse them. Again and again she has told me that it was unworthy of me to complain of want of popular success (that was not quite my real complaint, as you see, but I put it in that way sometimes). She assured me that she was a better judge of writing than I—in this case at least. She told me again and again that she had liked my articles before she cared for me; she gathered up all the compliments that she heard and used to produce them to me. I am so thin-skinned that I have given up reading any reviews of myself; intended praise often worries me, and I feel that, as I will not read abuse, I have no right to such compliments. She saw many reviews and, I presume, despised the unfavourable. But that is a trifle....This suggests to me one more remark....Had I fully succeeded and surpassed all my contemporaries in my own line, what should I have done? I should have written a book or two which might be read by my contemporaries and perhaps by the next generation, and which would have survived so long because they expressed a little better than others thoughts which were more or less common to thousands of people, many of them often a little less able than myself. Now I say, advisedly, that I do not think such an achievement as valuable as hers."

This is not the place in which to repeat the tribute of his love and bereavement; but you will find a discussion of the relative values of private virtues and intellectual achievement or public services in Leslie Stephen's last lecture on "Forgotten Benefactors" in *Social Rights and Duties*.

In the core of his emotional nature he gave preference to the private virtues. It is sometimes even disconcerting to find how much this influenced him in deciding the value of an author's works to the world. He is, as might have been anticipated, severe towards Rousseau; and in so far as he relents, it is due to his discovering in Rousseau "a redeeming quality", namely the value he set on the simple affections,

on "an idyllic life of calm domestic tranquil-
lity", perhaps not unlike Cowper's delight in
taking tea with Mrs Unwin, though streaked
(oddly as it appears to Stephen) with "a kind
of sensual appetite for pure simple pleasures".
In Hazlitt he cannot stomach the *Liber Amoris*;
in Coleridge, his having left Southey to look
after Mrs Coleridge and the children; and in
De Quincey he cannot overlook that the source
of the awe-struck sense of the vast and vague
which De Quincey communicated so mag-
nificently, was opium. In Thackeray, one of
his favourite novelists, he sees no faults that
seriously matter, since "his writings mean, if
they mean anything, that the love of a wife and
child and friends is the one sacred element in
our nature, of infinitely higher price than anything which can come into competition with
it; and that Vanity Fair is what it is because it
stimulates the pursuit of objects frivolous and
unsatisfying just so far that they imply in-
difference to those emotions". He is also
lenient to Kingsley, partly because he detects

in Kingsley the belief that "the root of all that is good in man lies in the purity and vigour of the domestic affections". In short, there are times when we are left wondering if a critic, in whom the exercise of the intellect was a passion, is not saying in effect: "Be good, sweet maid, and let who will be clever." There are passages scattered through his books which indicate that, compared with qualities of heart, all others seemed to him like a row of figures preceded by a decimal point and incapable of rising to the value of a single unit. That he underrated the value of his own work, there is no doubt. Even his masterly *English Thought in the Eighteenth Century* failed to satisfy him. He knew it was well done, but he doubted its value, since thought and imaginative literature were only by-products of social evolution, "the noise that the wheels make as they go round", and therefore no history of thought could be complete by itself. It was because Sainte-Beuve had taken such pains to place every author in his social setting and his times that he respected Sainte-Beuve's work so much. The view held in France by some critics, and advocated in England by Oscar Wilde and Walter Pater, that criticism was the quintessence of literature appeared to him too absurd to discuss. All the critic could do for his fellow-men was to stimulate their interest in literature by pointing out what he had himself enjoyed or not enjoyed, and by giving names to the qualities he perceived in them. He could appeal to the reader and say: Are not these, when you come to think it over, the strong points of this book, and these the weak ones?

Stephen himself was deficient in the power of transmitting the emotions he had derived himself from literature; he seldom, if ever, attempted to record a thrill. But he excelled in describing the qualities of authors, whether he summed up for or against them; and this is a most important part of the critic's function. By focussing in a phrase our scattered impressions, the critic confers an intellectual benefit which increases our interest when we think over an author's works. True, we can enjoy Defoe without noticing that his method of producing an impression of reality is the same as that of the circumstantial liar, who introduces details so fortuitous that it is hard to believe he could have invented them; but when Leslie Stephen says this, it brings suddenly together in our minds a number of instances. And the same effect is produced by his remark that knowledge of human nature in Fielding is based on observation rather than intuitive sympathy. Leslie Stephen's critical essays are crammed with illuminating comments of this kind. Of course, they do not help us to decide whether the fiction in question is good or bad, any more than a naturalist's description of a beast necessarily throws light on its value to man. But criticism must be in great part a Natural History of Authors, in which are set forth their distinctive features, their adaptation to their environment, and their relations to other species. When it comes to judgment, the test which Leslie Stephen applied was the relation of a work to life, the extent to which it ministered, in one way or another, to all human good.